An Evaluation of Biological Inventory Data Collected at Effigy Mounds National Monument
Vertebrate and Vascular Plant Inventories

Natural Resource Technical Report NPS/HTLN/NRTR—2009/256

Michael H. Williams
Kodge Data Services
150 Shady Branch
Benton, MO 63736

October 2009

U.S. Department of the Interior
National Park Service
Natural Resource Program Center
Fort Collins, Colorado

The National Park Service, Natural Resource Program Center publishes a range of reports that address natural resource topics of interest and applicability to a broad audience in the National Park Service and others in natural resource management, including scientists, conservation and environmental constituencies, and the public.

The Natural Resource Technical Report Series is used to disseminate results of scientific studies in the physical, biological, and social sciences for both the advancement of science and the achievement of the National Park Service mission. The series provides contributors with a forum for displaying comprehensive data that are often deleted from journals because of page limitations.

All manuscripts in the series receive the appropriate level of peer review to ensure that the information is scientifically credible, technically accurate, appropriately written for the intended audience, and designed and published in a professional manner. This report received informal peer review by subject-matter experts who were not directly involved in the collection, analysis, or reporting of the data.

Views, statements, findings, conclusions, recommendations, and data in this report are those of the author(s) and do not necessarily reflect views and policies of the National Park Service, U.S. Department of the Interior. Mention of trade names or commercial products does not constitute endorsement or recommendation for use by the National Park Service.

This report is available from http://science.nature.nps.gov/im/units/htln/ and the Natural Resource Publications Management website (http://www.nature.nps.gov/publications/NRPM/).

Please cite this publication as:

Williams, M. H. 2009. An evaluation of biological inventory data collected at Effigy Mounds National Monument: Vertebrate and vascular plant inventories. Natural Resource Technical Report NPS/HTLN/NRTR—2009/256. National Park Service, Fort Collins, Colorado.

NPS 394/100536, October 2009

Contents

Tables

Abstract

The Inventory and Monitoring program of the NPS provides twelve basic inventories for park managers, including lists of species that occur in NPS units. Eight hundred twelve species are certified on the list of vascular plants and vertebrates for Effigy Mounds National Monument (EFMO). Based on a review of the evidence, 733 (90%) species were categorized as Present in Park, and 79 (10%) as Probably Present. Four hundred ninety nine species were Unconfirmed, Encroaching, or Historic. In addition to documenting the presence of species, reviewers categorized the general abundance of 634 (86%) species and determined residency for all documented vertebrates with the exception of 16 fish. Species lists for EFMO can be queried from the Natural Resource Information Portal at http://nrinfo.nps.gov/Home.mvc.

Fifty nine non-native species are documented to occur in the park. Of these are four birds and 55 vascular plants. Non-native vascular plant species were assigned a NatureServe Invasive Species Impact Rank (I-Rank) based on impact to native species and natural biodiversity. Eleven of the 55 (20%) non-native plants found on EFMO received an overall I-Rank score that included the high category (i.e. most threatening).

A total of 56 species are listed by the Iowa Department of Natural Resources as a species of conservation status. The federally listed endangered least tern is listed as unconfirmed at EFMO. The federally listed endangered least tern was noted as unconfirmed on EFMO. Twenty nine state listed species include five threatened species documented on EFMO (burbot, western sand darter, least shrew, Southern bog lemming, golden corydalis), one noted as probably present (long eared owl), and eight noted as unconfirmed (Blanding's turtle, central newt, creeping juniper, glandular wood fern, Henslow's sparrow, jeweled shooting star, leathery grapefern, wild lupine). Five state listed endangered species were documented on EFMO (bald eagle, northern harrier, peregrine falcon, red shouldered hawk, weed shiner), two noted as probably present (lake sturgeon, spotted skunk), and eight noted as unconfirmed (arrow arum, king rail, massasauga rattlesnake, short eared owl, swamp-loosestrife, waxy meadowrue, winterberry, wood turtle). Future inventory efforts are discussed.

Acknowledgements

Thanks go to the inventory project researchers and their many volunteers including: Jon Stravers, Audubon Upper Mississippi River Campaign, McGregor, IA; Evelyn Howell and Joie Stolt, University of Wisconsin-Madison. Additional thanks go to NPS personnel including Park, Heartland Network, Midwest Region, and Washington Office staff. A special thanks to the staff of Effigy Mounds National Monument for allowing access to the park during inventory and monitoring efforts.

Introduction

As part of the National Park Service's effort to "improve park management through greater reliance on scientific knowledge," a primary role of the Inventory and Monitoring (I&M) Program is to collect, organize, and make available natural resource data. A list of species known to occur in NPS units is considered a basic inventory need (see: http://science.nature.nps.gov/im/inventory/index.cfm). The I&M Program's Heartland Network (HTLN) recently completed inventories of vertebrate species and vascular plants at Effigy Mounds National Monument (EFMO). In doing so, all existing data were cataloged, targeted field investigations were conducted, and species lists were certified by taxonomic experts. The primary goal of these efforts was to document at least 90% of the vertebrate and vascular plant species believed to occur in the park. This report provides a summary of results.

Methods

The HTLN followed a strategic plan of action set forth in an Inventory Study Plan (Boetsch et al. 2000) to complete inventories of vascular plants and vertebrate species. This plan was instigated by the Natural Resource Challenge in response to the National Parks Omnibus Management Act of 1998 and adheres to the requisite approaches delineated in Guidelines for Biological Inventories (NPS 1999) and the recommendations of the Service-wide I&M Program. The Inventory Study Plan identified steps to conduct a natural resource "information assessment" of existing park data. These steps included (1) developing master lists of species known or expected to occur in the park, (2) conducting field inventories, and (3) certifying the resultant species data.

> The term species (as opposed to organism) is generically used throughout this report to refer to unique taxa at the species level or below.

Expected Species Lists

In order to determine the completeness of inventory information, the HTLN developed lists of vascular plants and vertebrates expected to occur in the park. The master list of fish was supplied by Martin Conrad, Fisheries Biologist, Iowa Department of Natural Resources. The master list of birds was derived from range maps in The Golden Guide, A Guide To Field Identification Of North American Birds (Robbins et al. 1983), and National Geographic Society's Field Guide To The Birds Of North America (1987). Expected amphibians were derived from the U.S. amphibian distribution map internet site at http://home.bsu.edu/~00MJLANNOO/USamphibians.html. The range maps of Conant and Collins (1998) "A Field Guide to Reptiles and Amphibians of Eastern and Central North America" used to derive expected reptile species lists. Any problems associated with synonymy were resolved by following Conant and Collins (1998). Bowles' (1975) Distribution and Biogeography of Mammals of Iowa was used to develop the mammal list. An initial compilation and evaluation of park floras was completed by Dr. Jim Bennett, National Wildlife Health Center, USGS BRD (Bennett 1995). Bennett compiled floras from "numerous sources: park lists, published journal articles and books, vegetation surveys, natural history reports, herbarium lists, park files and memoranda, and other miscellaneous park reports." Species names were standardized to USDA PLANTS (1999) and inconsistencies in infraspecific designations were resolved on a case-by-case basis.

Compiling Existing Inventory Data

Concurrent with development of expected species lists, HTLN staff worked with technical support from the Natural Resource Program Center (NRPC) to consolidate existing inventories. HTLN staff searched for existing inventory data, extracted species lists from the reports, labeled the lists with appropriate reference information, and forwarded the data to NRPC for processing.

HTLN staff mined inventory data from regional inventory databases, and transferred the network's Flora database. Staff also assembled bibliographic data concerning the primary park inventories. The Procite bibliographic database, NatureBib (aka NRBIB), was queried to produce an initial list of references. The lists were reviewed to ensure that each inventory: 1) included primary, rather than secondary, inventory data; 2) was based on observed, not expected, occurrences; and 3) was the result of professional surveys or research, rather than amateur observations. Park resource managers then reviewed and added to the lists.

HTLN staff searched for references to botanical collections as sources of species occurrence records. The process of searching regional herbaria for pertinent species records then commenced. The primary objectives were: 1) to find previously unknown collections; and 2) to document the current repository for older, known collections. The HTLN initiated a cooperative agreement with the National Wildlife Health Center (Biological Resources Division) to conduct computerized searches of regional and national museums and herbaria for park records of vertebrate and vascular plant occurrences. Given the limited timeframe, repositories with searchable collections databases were used. Dr. Jim Bennett, author of a summary of Midwestern NPS floras (Bennett 1995), was the principal investigator and was assisted with results of a search of the EFMO ANCS+ database collection provided by the HTLN.

> ANCS+ is a database management system developed by NPS to accession and catalog its museum collections.

The NPSpecies Database

NPSpecies is a master database for documenting the occurrence and status of all organisms in NPS units. The database includes standardized information associated with the occurrence of species, including scientific names and their synonyms (i.e. a local list or a standard list of species names), common names, abundance, residency, nativity, T&E status, and notes of particular management interest to a park. NPSpecies supports NPS staff and collaborators at the park, network, regional, and national levels by managing fundamental park-level species information, and making this information available to other applications and databases for more specialized analyses. A primary purpose for NPSpecies is to provide park managers, planners, and scientists with basic information on species occurrences and status for making decisions and working with other agencies, the scientific community, and the public for the long-term protection of park ecosystems (NPSpecies 2009).

Within NPSpecies, each species record is supported by evidence in the form of voucher specimens, references (scientific reports or datasets), and/or observation records that document the occurrence of the species in the park. Historical and currently-accepted scientific names from multiple taxonomic classification systems are cross-referenced using taxonomic standards (e.g., the Integrated Taxonomic Information System and the USDA PLANTS database) to allow for data integration and sharing across parks and with other agencies and organizations. In addition, parks are able to produce species lists based on the taxonomic authorities that are most accepted in their region and by their partner agencies.

Populating NPSpecies focused on three objectives: 1) transferring existing data; 2) including evidence for each record; and 3) verifying the accuracy of lists. As master species lists were compiled and transferred into NPSpecies a conservative approach was taken while assigning park status (e.g. present, probably present, etc.) to ensure that assessments of completeness were based on verifiable records. Many records imported from previous databases were unsubstantiated (i.e. not linked to a verifiable data source) and were classified as unconfirmed. Verification of vertebrate taxa was conducted by comparing digital records to original sources. The process proved valuable for assuring data quality as transcription errors, spelling mistakes, erroneous names, and synonymy problems were identified and corrected. In the process, park status (e.g. present in park, probable, unconfirmed) were also updated. After verifying and

3

updating, any remaining species without evidence were assigned an 'unconfirmed' status. Reliable status information is necessary to generate verifiable species lists for use in assessing inventory completeness. WASO I&M then completed the processing of these data and returned an NPSpecies database.

Inventories

Targeted field inventories were conducted to augment existing inventory data while addressing information gaps and high priority information needs. Two workshops were held during FY 2000 to assist in determining and prioritizing inventory needs (see appendix F in Boetsch et al. 2000). Regional taxa experts participated in these workshops and helped to revise project plans and priorities, and develop a greater awareness of taxa-specific inventory methods.

Subsequent to these initial steps, the HTLN began implementing inventories of amphibians and reptiles, birds, fish, mammals, and vascular plants. When completed, inventory reports were submitted to the HTLN and, once finalized, bibliographic data and the final report were uploaded to NatureBib. Species data (ie. taxonomic name, park status, abundance, etc.) and voucher data were uploaded to NPSpecies. Primary inventory data (ie. locations, events, etc.) and inventory specific data (i.e. bird counts, amphibian observations, etc.) were entered in a Microsoft (MS) Access database standardized to the current natural resource database template (NRDT) and uploaded to the NPS Data Store.

Inventory Certification

To support the objective of documenting 90% of vertebrate and vascular plant species expected to occur, subject matter experts (i.e. those involved with EFMO inventories) participated in the NPSpecies certification of taxonomic and attribute data for each taxa list. The process of certification is a data validation and quality assurance procedure for species checklists performed by subject matter experts most familiar with a particular taxonomic category. Taxon nomenclature are documented as well as park status, abundance, residency, and nativity.

Amphibian, reptile, and mammal certifications were compiled by James Christiansen, Drake University, Des Moines, IA. Bird certifications were conducted by Jon Stravers, Audubon Upper Mississippi River Campaign, McGregor, IA. Fish certifications were compiled by Scott Gritters, Iowa Department of Natural Resources. Vascular plant certifications were conducted by Evelyn Howell, University of Wisconsin-Madison. Generally, species lists were distributed as MS Excel worksheets and returned with revisions. Revised expected species lists containing a species park status (present, probably present, etc), abundance (common, uncommon, rare, etc), residency (breeder, resident, etc), and nativity as well as other attribute details were then updated (where necessary) via the desktop NPSpecies to reflect the current species' park status. These lists were then uploaded to the master online version of NPSpecies.

Results

Twenty four references (see Appendix 1) and 391 vouchers led to the certification of 812 species (NPSpecies 2009). In total, 733 species were categorized as Present in Park and 79 as Probably Present (Table 1). Additionally, 499 species were categorized as Unconfirmed, Encroaching, or Historic. Unconfirmed species were ranked as such due to weak evidence supporting their existence on the park.

Currently 56% of the species on the park's species list are documented (i.e., categorized as Present in Park). If species listed as Present in Park and Probably Present are included in the calculation, the percentage of documented species rises to 62%.

Table 1. Count of species by park status categories at EFMO (NPSpecies 2009).

Park Status[1]	Bird	Fish	Mammal	Amphibian	Reptile	Vascular Plant	Total
Present in Park	178	84	22	8	15	426	733
Probably Present	42	9	21	1	6		79
Encroaching						1	1
Unconfirmed	81	5		2	4	405	497
Historic				1			1
Total	301	98	43	12	25	832	1,311

[1] Refer to the Appendix for definitions of Park Status categories.

Of the 733 species documented as present, reviewers assigned a general abundance category (e.g., common, rare, etc.) to 634 (86%) (Table 2). Reviewers believed additional information was needed before an abundance category could be assigned to the remaining 99 (14%) species. Results are available to NPS staff through the Natural Resource Information Portal at http://nrinfo.nps.gov/Home.mvc. The portal is the product of the Integration of Resource Management Applications (IRMA) project. To learn more see: http://www1.nrintra.nps.gov/im/datamgmt/docs/IRMA_ProjectBrief_v1.0.pdf.

Residency values (e.g., breeder, migrant, resident, etc.) were assigned for all documented vertebrates with the exception of 16 fish that were categorized as unknown. Unknown residency values were assigned primarily because it was unclear as to whether or not the species bred on the park. Non-natives documented to occur in the park (i.e., Present in Park) total 59. Of these are four birds and 55 vascular plants.

NatureServe, in cooperation with The Nature Conservancy and NPS, developed a protocol to rank the impact of non-native invasive vascular plants (Morse et al. 2004). Through a series of standardized questions, non-native species are evaluated and assigned an Invasive Species Impact Rank (I-Rank) based on impact to native species and natural biodiversity. I-Ranks are categorized as high, medium, low, or insignificant. Eleven of the 55 (20%) non-native plants found on EFMO received an overall I-Rank score that included the high category (Table 3). All are known to occur in the park (i.e., Present in Park).

A total of fifty six species (Table 4) are listed by the Iowa Department of Natural Resources as a species of conservation status. Additional NatureServe global, national, and subnational ranking status is provided. The federally listed endangered least tern (*Sterna antillarum*) was noted as unconfirmed on EFMO. Twenty nine state listed species include five threatened species documented on EFMO (burbot, *Lota lota*, western sand darter, *Ammocrypta clara*, least shrew, *Cryptotis parva*, Southern bog lemming, *Synaptomys cooperi*, golden corydalis, *Corydalus aureus*), one noted as probably present (long eared owl, *Asio otus*), and eight noted as unconfirmed (Blanding's turtle, *Emydoidea blandingii*, central newt, *Notophthalmus viridescens louisianensis*, creeping juniper, *Juniperus horizontalis*, glandular wood fern, *Dryopteris intermedia*, Henslow's sparrow, *Ammodramus henslowii*, jeweled shooting star, *Dodecatheon amethystinum*, leathery grapefern, *Botrychium multifidum*, wild lupine, *Lupinus perennis*). Five state listed endangered species were documented on EFMO (bald eagle, *Haliaeetus leucocephalus*, northern harrier, *Circus cyaneus*, peregrine falcon, *Falco peregrinus*, red shouldered hawk, *Buteo lineatus*, weed shiner, *Notropis texanus*), two noted as probably present (lake sturgeon, *Acipenser fulvescens*, spotted skunk, *Spilogale putorius*), and eight noted as unconfirmed (arrow arum, *Peltandra virginica*, king rail, *Rallus elegans*, massasauga rattlesnake, *Sistrurus catenatus*, short eared owl, *Asio flammeus*, swamp-loosestrife, *Decodon verticillatus*, waxy meadowrue, *Thalictrum revolutum*, winterberry, *Ilex verticillata*, wood turtle, *Clemmys insculpta*).

.

Table 2. Count of species by abundance categories at EFMO (NPSpecies 2009).

Abundance Category[1]	Bird	Fish	Mammal	Amphibian	Reptile	Vascular Plant	Total
Abundant	5		13	8	8	29	63
Common	121	42				72	235
Uncommon	47	14				182	243
Rare	4	5	2		2	79	92
Occasional	1						1
Unknown		23	7		5	64	99
Total	178	84	22	8	15	426	733

[1] Refer to the Appendix for definitions of Park Status categories.

Table 3. Non-native plants, occurring on EFMO, with an Invasive Species Impact Rank (I-Rank) containing high.

Scientific Name	Common Name	Overall I-Rank	Ecological Impact[1]	Management Difficulty[2]	I-Rank Reasons Summary[3]
Alliaria petiolata	Garlic mustard	High / Medium	Medium / Low	Medium	Widespread, but commonly in highly disturbed systems. Recent evidence points garlic mustard starting to invade a greater range of geographic and ecological areas, including intact, healthy ecosystems.
Berberis thunbergii	Japanese barberry	High / Medium	High / Medium	Insignificant	Although it was initially thought to invade mostly disturbed sites (old fields, roadsides, etc.) it is now known to invade high quality habitats.
Bromus inermis	Smooth brome	High / Medium	Medium	Medium	A threat to prairie and grasslands in the Midwest; alters rate of natural succession; changes native species composition; highly persistent.
Carduus nutans	Nodding thistle	High / Low	Medium / Insignificant	High / Medium	Persistent in open areas, including prairies, grasslands, roadsides and areas of disturbance in dense woods; prolific seed production; seeds viable for up to 15 years.
Cirsium arvense	Creeping thistle	High / Medium	Medium / Low	High / Medium	Widespread, well recognized non-native that is on the majority of states' noxious species lists.
Elymus repens	Creeping wild rye	High / Medium	Medium / Low	High / Medium	This species is widespread occurring in nearly every U.S. state but local expansion is still occurring particularly in the western states. Negative impacts are significant as this species has the potential to form dense, monospecific stands.
Lonicera tatarica	Tatarian honeysuckle	High / Medium	Medium	Medium	Although not as impactful as some of the other *Lonicera* species, this species exhibits some canopy disturbance reducing species richness and abundance and inhibiting native tree seedlings. Negative impacts on community composition and native species.
Morus alba	White mulberry	High / Medium	Medium / Low	Medium / Low	Distributed throughout most of the U.S.; spread by birds and mammals; moderate capability of invading undisturbed areas.

8

Table 3 (cont.). Non-native plants, occurring on EFMO, with an Invasive Species Impact Rank (I-Rank) containing high.

Scientific Name	Common Name	Overall I-Rank	Ecological Impact[1]	Management Difficulty[2]	I-Rank Reasons Summary[3]
Phalaris arundinacea	Reed canarygrass	High	High	High / Medium	This species can form dense, persistent, monotypic stands of creeping rhizomes in a thick sod layer in wetlands, moist meadows and riparian areas.
Poa compressa	Canada bluegrass	High / Low	Medium / Low	High / Medium	Widespread in the U.S. in disturbed areas, prairies, and ridgetop woodlands; may crowd out native species; forms large colonies; spreads very quickly; control is difficult.
Rhamnus cathartica	Common buckthorn	High / Medium	Medium	Medium	Widespread across the continental U.S.; can form even-aged, dense thickets shading out natives and often obliterating them; suppresses fire in fire-adapted communities.

[1] Subcategory of Overall I-Rank specifically addressing species negative impacts on native plant/animal populations/communities.
[2] Subcategory of Overall I-Rank specifically addressing difficulty of control.
[3] Summary reasons for NatureServe Overall I-Rank. For more information see the NatureServe Species Explorer at http://www.natureserve.org. These summaries reflective of NatureServe data last updated 6 February, 2009.

Table 4. Species on the park's local list which possess a state heritage program rank and/or other designated conservation status (State Heritage Conservation Rank/Status, Global, National, Subnational, and/or a Federal Status).

Amphibian	Scientific Name	Park Status[1]	State Heritage Program Status[2]	Federal Status[3]	Global / National / Subnational Status[4]	Global Short Term Trend[4]
Central newt	Notophthalmus viridescens louisianensis	Unconfirmed	Threatened		G5 / N5 / S2	Stable to increasing
Bird						
Bald eagle	Haliaeetus leucocephalus	Present in Park	Endangered		G5 / N5B,N5N / S3B,S3N	Stable to increasing
Black tern	Chlidonias niger	Present in Park	Special Concern		G4 / N4B / S1B,S4N	Severely to rapidly declining
Forster's tern	Sterna forsteri	Present in Park	Special Concern		G5 / N5B,N5N / S2B,S3N	
Henslow's sparrow	Ammodramus henslowii	Unconfirmed	Threatened		G4 / N3B,N4N / S3B,S2N	Severely declining
King rail	Rallus elegans	Unconfirmed	Endangered		G4 / N4B,N4N / S1N	Rapidly declining to declining
Least tern	Sterna antillarum	Unconfirmed	Endangered	Endangered	G4 / N4B / S1	Declining
Long-eared owl	Asio otus	Probably Present	Threatened		G5 / N5B,N5N / S2B,S3N	Trends difficult to ascertain
Northern harrier	Circus cyaneus	Present in Park	Endangered		G5 / N5B,N5N / S2B,S4N	Stable
Peregrine falcon	Falco peregrinus	Present in Park	Endangered		G4 / N4B,N4N / S1B	Increasing
Red-shouldered hawk	Buteo lineatus	Present in Park	Endangered		G5 / N5B,N5N / S2B	Stable to increasing
Short eared owl	Asio flammeus	Unconfirmed	Endangered		G5 / N5B,N5N / S1B,S2N	Declining (decline of 10-30%)
Fish						
Burbot	Lota lota	Present in Park	Threatened		G5 / N5 / S3	
Lake sturgeon	Acipenser fulvescens	Probably Present	Endangered		G3 / N3N4 / S1	Stable

Table 4 (cont.). Species on the park's local list which possess a state heritage program rank and/or other designated conservation status (State Heritage Conservation Rank/Status, Global, National, Subnational, and/or a Federal Status).

	Scientific Name	Park Status[1]	State Heritage Program Status[2]	Federal Status[3]	Global / National / Subnational Status[4]	Global Short Term Trend[4]
Fish						
Weed shiner	*Notropis texanus*	Present in Park	Endangered		G5 / N5 / S2	Has declined in the north.
Western sand darter	*Ammocrypta clara*	Present in Park	Threatened		G3 / N3 / S2	
Mammal						
Least shrew	*Cryptotis parva*	Present in Park	Threatened		G5 / N5 / S2	
Southern bog lemming	*Synaptomys cooperi*	Present in Park	Threatened		G5 / N5 / S3	
Southern flying squirrel	*Glaucomys volans*	Present in Park	Special Concern		G5 / N5 / S4	
Spotted skunk	*Spilogale putorius*	Probably Present	Endangered		G5 / N5 / S1	
Reptile						
Blanding's turtle	*Emydoidea blandingii*	Unconfirmed	Threatened		G4 / N4 / S3	Declining to stable
Massasauga rattlesnake	*Sistrurus catenatus*	Unconfirmed	Endangered		G3 / N3N4 / S1	Declining to stable
Smooth green snake	*Opheodrys vernalis*	Unconfirmed	Special Concern		G5 / N5 / S3	Stable
Wood turtle	*Clemmys insculpta*	Unconfirmed	Endangered		G4 / N4 / S1	Declining
Vascular Plants						
Annual ground cherry	*Physalis pubescens*	Unconfirmed	Special Concern		G5 / N4? / SH	
Arrow arum	*Peltandra virginica*	Unconfirmed	Endangered		G5 / N5 / S1	
Balsam fir	*Abies balsamea*	Unconfirmed	Special Concern		G5 / N5 / S1	

Table 4 (cont.). Species on the park's local list which possess a state heritage program rank and/or other designated conservation status (State Heritage Conservation Rank/Status, Global, National, Subnational, and/or a Federal Status).

Vascular Plants	Scientific Name	Park Status[1]	State Heritage Program Status[2]	Federal Status[3]	Global / National / Subnational Status[4]	Global Short Term Trend[4]
Burreed	*Sparganium androcladum*	Present in Park	Special Concern		G4 / NNR / S1	
Coast blite	*Chenopodium rubrum*	Unconfirmed	Special Concern		G5 / N3N5 / SH	
Creeping juniper	*Juniperus horizontalis*	Unconfirmed	Threatened		G5 / N5 / S1	
Dewberry	*Rubus hispidus*	Unconfirmed	Special Concern		G5 / NNR / SU	
Dwarf spikerush	*Eleocharis parvula*	Unconfirmed	Special Concern		G5 / N3N5 / SH	
Glandular wood fern	*Dryopteris intermedia*	Unconfirmed	Threatened		G5 / N5 / S1	
Golden corydalis	*Corydalis aurea*	Present in Park	Threatened		G5 / NNR / S2	
Hairy Solomon's-seal	*Polygonatum pubescens*	Unconfirmed	Special Concern		G5 / NNR / S2	
Jeweled shooting star	*Dodecatheon amethystinum*	Unconfirmed	Threatened		G4 / N4 / S2	
Large-leaved pondweed	*Potamogeton amplifolius*	Unconfirmed	Special Concern		G5 / NNR / S1	
Leathery grapefern	*Botrychium multifidum*	Unconfirmed	Threatened		G5 / NNR / S2	
Mud plantain	*Heteranthera limosa*	Unconfirmed	Special Concern		G5 / N4N5 / SH	
Naked mitrewort	*Mitella nuda*	Present in Park	Special Concern		G5 / NNR / S1	
Pawpaw	*Asimina triloba*	Unconfirmed	Special Concern		G5 / N5 / S2	
Purple angelica	*Angelica atropurpurea*	Present in Park	Special Concern		G5 / NNR / S3	
Purple coneflower	*Echinacea purpurea*	Unconfirmed	Special Concern		G4 / N4 / S2	Declining

12

Table 4 (cont.). Species on the park's local list which possess a state heritage program rank and/or other designated conservation status (State Heritage Conservation Rank/Status, Global, National, Subnational, and/or a Federal Status).

Vascular Plants	Scientific Name	Park Status[1]	State Heritage Program Status[2]	Federal Status[3]	Global / National / Subnational Status[4]	Global Short Term Trend[4]
Rough bedstraw	Galium asprellum	Present in Park	Special Concern		G5 / NNR / S2	
Sassafras	Sassafras albidum	Unconfirmed	Special Concern		G5 / N5 / SU	
Soft rush	Juncus effusus	Unconfirmed	Special Concern		G5 / N5 / S2	
Summer grape	Vitis aestivalis	Present in Park	Special Concern		G5 / N5 / S2	
Swamp rose	Rosa palustris	Unconfirmed	Special Concern		G5 / NNR / S1	
Swamp thistle	Cirsium muticum	Present in Park	Special Concern		G5 / N5 / S2	
Swamp-loosestrife	Decodon verticillatus	Unconfirmed	Endangered		G5 / NNR / S1	
Water milfoil	Myriophyllum verticillatum	Unconfirmed	Special Concern		G5 / NNR / S1	
Waxy meadowrue	Thalictrum revolutum	Unconfirmed	Endangered		G5 / NNR / S1	
White-stemmed pondweed	Potamogeton praelongus	Unconfirmed	Special Concern		G5 / NNR / S1	
Widgeon grass	Ruppia maritima	Unconfirmed	Special Concern		G5 / N4N5 / S1	
Wild lupine	Lupinus perennis	Unconfirmed	Threatened		G5 / N3N5 / S1	
Winterberry	Ilex verticillata	Unconfirmed	Endangered		G5 / N5 / S1	

[1] Refer to the Appendix for definitions of Park Status categories.
[2] The official endangerment status the Iowa Department of Natural Resources has assigned to this species. (http://www.iowadnr.com/other/threatened.html).
[3] U.S. Endangered Species Act: Current status of the taxon as designated or proposed by the U.S. Fish and Wildlife Service (USFWS), and as reported in the U.S. Federal Register in accordance with the U.S. Endangered Species Act of 1973, as amended.

The NatureServe conservation status, developed by NatureServe and its network of member (state) programs, of a species from a state/province perspective, characterizing the relative imperilment of the species. G = global (rounded), N = national, and S = subnational; 1 = critically imperiled, 2 = imperiled, 3 = vulnerable, 4 = apparently secure, 5 = secure; B=Breeding population, NR=Not rated. Refer to http://www.natureserve.org/explorer/ranking.htm#interpret for additional information on conservation status ranks.

Discussion

The NPS Inventory Strategic Plan states that "the ultimate goal is to establish an accurate inventory of all life forms within a park..." (NPS 2009, see also NPS 1992). The HTLN supports this goal by documenting over 80% of all vertebrates and vascular plants known to occur at EFMO. One result of these efforts is the compilation of reliable species lists. These lists, however sound, should always be considered incomplete. Inventory lists will change as new information about species distributions becomes available. The overall number of species designated as Present in Park or Probably Present is similar to similarly sized parks in the HTLN (Table 5).

Table 5. Number of species designated as present in park or probably present in HTLN parks (NPSpecies 2009).

Park	Bird	Fish	Mammal	Amphibian	Reptile	Vascular Plants	TOTALS	Park Size (ac.)
EFMO	220	93	43	9	21	426	812	1,481
HOME	81	31	41	6	9	304	472	160
HEHO	120	28	45	1	11	230	435	186
LIBO	224	-	38	13	13	332	620	200
GWCA	192	34	44	8	17	662	957	210
HOCU	274	15	40	21	25	457	832	280
PIPE	252	20	31	6	6	557	872	282
ARPO	111	65	33	17	40	332	598	389
WICR	134	53	48	11	31	569	846	1,750
PERI	74	41	44	21	36	665	881	4,300
HOSP	114	52	49	22	45	910	1,192	5,549
TAPR	136	29	42	8	27	456	698	10,894
CUVA	241	65	37	19	21	1,167	1,550	32,859
OZAR	167	122	55	29	45	880	1,298	82,196
BUFF	211	78	58	22	43	1,353	1,765	95,730

Future Inventory Efforts

While significant strides have been made in documenting the presence of vertebrate species and vascular plants, it is anticipated that additional survey efforts will be required to increase the number of documented species (i.e. Present in Park). For example, about half of the birds, mammals, and reptiles are listed as probably present or unconfirmed and lack adequate documentation. Additionally, several state listed species are listed as probably present or unconfirmed. If species are thought to be Probably Present or Unconfirmed, follow-up surveys (perhaps targeted inventories?) are warranted or existing monitoring programs broadened to include searches for these species. Additional follow up inventories coupled with habitat studies may document their presence.

Reviewers assigned a general abundance category for all but 99 of the documented species (23 fish, seven mammals, five reptiles, and 64 vascular plants). Reviewers also assigned a residency value for all but 16. Continued monitoring of the species may provide for updated abundance and residency.

Based on the results of the data reported herein, future inventory recommendations include:

- additional resources to survey for species listed in Table 4,
- coupled with the above, focus on species listed as Probably Present, Unconfirmed, and Historic,

Key Findings of Management Interest

- The bird inventory (Stravers et al. 2003) found several species of special interest that included the red-shouldered hawk (*Buteo lineatus*), bald eagle (*Haliaeetus leucocephalus*), and acadian flycatcher (*Empidonax virescens*). The park has been dedicated as a Bird Conservation Area by the Iowa Department of Natural Resource Wildlife Diversity Section, and also listed as an Important Bird Area by the National Audubon Society.

- The red shouldered hawk report (Stravers 2003) confirmed nesting in three sites in 2002 and four sites in 2003. Two additional sites that are adjacent to National Park Service property were suspected nesting sites. Total reproductive success for red-shoulder nesting attempts within the park for 2002 & 2003 was seven nesting attempts, three successful, with four nestlings reaching fledging age. Previous observations of study areas along the Yellow River and Sny Magill Slough within EFMO have had some of the highest densities of nesting red-shouldered hawks on the Upper Mississippi River.

- The vascular plant inventory (Stolt and Howell 2005) indicated that the forest communities of the original property (the North Unit, South Unit and Sny Magill) have not undergone much change in species richness or community structure since a previous survey conducted in 1982-83 by Howell et al. (1983). The most dramatic change occurred in the Oak Hickory Forest, which is situated in the northern part of the North Unit, where ground layer species richness appears to have more than doubled.

Literature Cited

Bennett, J. P. 1995. Floristic summary of 22 Midwestern national parks. Wisconsin Cooperative Park Studies Unit, USGS, BRD.

Boetsch, J., M. DeBacker, P. Hughes, D. Peitz, L. Thomas, G. Wagner, and B. Witcher. 2000. A study plan to inventory vascular plants and vertebrates: Heartland Network. National Park Service.

Bowles, J. B. 1975. Distribution and biogeography of mammals of Iowa. Special publications the museum. Texas Tech University, 9: 184pp.

Conant, R. and J. T. Collins. 1998. Reptiles and amphibians: eastern/central North America. Houghton Mifflin. Boston, Massachusetts.

Howell, E., D. Morrison, and G. Moore. 1983. A vegetation survey of Effigy Mounds NM, Iowa.

Morse, L. E., J. M. Randall, N. Benton, R. Hiebert, and S. Lu. 2004. An invasive species assessment protocol: Evaluating non-native plants for their impact on biodiversity. Version 1. NatureServe, Arlington, Virginia.

National Geographic Society. 1987. Field guide to the birds of North America. Washington, D.C. National Geographic Society. 464 p.

National Park Service. 1992. NPS-75: Natural resources inventory and monitoring guideline. National Park Service, Inventory and Monitoring Program.

National Park Service. 1999. Guidelines for biological inventories. Inventory and Monitoring Program, National Park Service. 10 pp.

National Park Service. 2009. Strategic plan for natural resource inventories, FY 2008 – FY 2012. Natural Resource Report NPS/NRPC/NRR—2009/094. National Park Service, Fort Collins, Colorado.

NPSpecies Proper: NPSpecies - The National Park Service biodiversity database. Secure online version. https://science1.nature.nps.gov/npspecies/web/main/start. Accessed May, 2009.

Robbins, C. S., Bruun, B., and H. S. Zim. 1983. A guide to field identification of North American birds. Western Publishing Co. Racine, Wisconsin.

Stolt, J. L. and E. Howell. 2005. Inventory of forest structure and diversity at Effigy Mounds National Monument. Technical Report NPS/HTLN/EFMO/J6370030956.

Stravers, J. W. 2003. Report on red-shouldered hawk inventories at Effigy Mounds National Monument – 2002 & 2003. National Park Service.

Stravers, J. W., McKay, K. J., and T. McClanahan. 2003. Avian surveys at Effigy Mounds National Monument. Technical report NPS/HTLN/P6370020493.

USDA. 1999. The PLANTS database (http://plants.usda.gov/plants). National Plant Data Center, Baton Rouge, Louisiana.

Appendix 1. NPSpecies bibliographic references for EFMO.

Author unknown. 1991. USFWS/EFMO BIRD CHECKLIST. The original citation from NPSpecies = USFWS/EFMO BIRD CHECKLIST,1991.

Author unknown. 1997. Bird checklist of Effigy Mounds NM. In: B. Collins, F. Lesher, B. Voelker, B. Zarwell and R. Zarwell. Migratory bird survey checklist of Effigy Mounds NM. Brian Collins.

Bennett, J. P. 1993. Flora of Effigy Mounds National Monument. University Of Wisconsin – Madison, Madison, Wisconsin.

Blewett, T. J. 1986. A vegetation survey of grasslands and rare plants of Effigy Mounds NM.

Boetsch, J., M. DeBacker, P. Hughes, D. Peitz, L. Thomas, G. Wagner and B. Witcher. 2000. Inventory Study Plan. in Author unknown. A study plan to inventory vascular plants and vertebrates: Heartland Network.

Bohr, J. 1979. Seed flora of Effigy Mounds NM. An update of cirea 1950 herbarium index.

Carter, D. 1996. Field reports of birds at Effigy Mounds National Monument. National Park Service, Harpers Ferry, Iowa.

Christiansen, J. L. 1999. Survey for amphibisans, reptiles, and small mammals at Effigy Mounds National Monument, US Fish and Wildlife Refuge.

Christiansen, J. L. 2000. Final report: Survey for amphibians, reptiles, and small mammals at Effigy Mounds National Monument.

Gritters, S. 2004. Fish species list for EFMO. In author unknown. Fish species list for EFMO. Fish species list reviewed and commented.

Hop, K., S. Lubinski, and S. Menard. 2005. Vegetation mapping program. Effigy Mounds National Monument, Iowa. A cooperative effort between the National Park Service, U.S. Geological Survey, and the Minneapolis Office of NatureServe.

Howell, E. 2005. Inventory of forest structure and diversity at Effigy Mounds National Monument. Technical Report NPS/HTLN/EFMO/J6370030956.

Howell, E. A., D. G. Morrison, and G. F. Moore. 1983. A vegetation of Effigy Mounds National Monument. Document located in inventory spring 1997.

Moore, G. F. 1988. Plant communities of Effigy Mounds National Monument and their relationship to presettlement regional vegetation. University Of Wisconsin - Madison. Document located in inventory spring 1997.

Munson. 1991. Letter. The original citation from NPSpecies = MUNSON, EFMO MEMO, 1991.

Nichols, S. J., J. Allen, B. Black, and B. Kennedy. 2002. Status of freshwater unionid populations at Effigy Mounds National Monument, 2002.

NPS, Heartland Network. 2005. EFMO general bird inventory dataset. Dataset.

NPS, Heartland Network. 2005. EFMO red-shouldered hawk geodatabase. Dataset ( ). ProductID: 1666 NPS MWR GIS Service Center.

NPS, Heartland Network. 2006. EFMO vascular plant database. Dataset ( ).

Sanchini, P. 1999. Assessment of wetland habitats near ponds at Effigy Mounds National Monument.

Schablilon, J. 1965. Effigy Mounds National Monument plant species list. National Park Service, Harpers Ferry, Iowa. Checklist.

Stravers, J. 2004. Report on red-shouldered hawk inventories at Effigy Mounds National Monument 2002 & 2003. Technical report NPS/HTLN/PMIS/EFMO. PMIS #070638.

Stravers, J. and K. McKay. 2004. Avian surveys at Effigy Mounds National Monument. Technical report NPS/HTLN/P6370020493.

Stubbendieck, J., C. H. Butterfield, and T. R. Flessner. 1992. An assessment of exotic plants within Great Plains parks of the Midwest region. University Of Nebraska, Lincoln, Nebraska. Document located in inventory spring 1997.

Appendix 2. NPSpecies Data Dictionary

Park Status	The current status of each species in each park.	Applicable only to organisms with the *Local List* checkbox checked. The possible values reflect a combination of confidence, and availability and currency of verifiable evidence in NPSpecies.
Present in Park	Species' occurrence in park is documented and assumed to be extant.	Extremely high confidence that the species is currently in the park. A current, verifiable reference, voucher, or observation is included in NPSpecies.
Probably Present	Park is within species' range and contains appropriate habitat. Documented occurrences of the species in the adjoining region of the park give reason to suspect that it probably occurs within the park. The degree of probability may vary within this category, including species that range from common to rare.	Very high confidence that the organism is currently in the park. Verifiable evidence may exist in NPSpecies, but is not considered current enough to elevate the status to Present in Park. Efforts should be made to obtain current, verifiable evidence in NPSpecies to elevate the Park Status to "Present in Park". If reasonable efforts to obtain current, verifiable evidence are unsuccessful, then the Park Status should be changed to Unconfirmed, Historic, Encroaching, or False Report as applicable.
Unconfirmed	Included for the park based on weak ("unconfirmed record") or no evidence, giving minimal indication of the species' occurrence in the park.	Any confidence from very low to high that the organism is currently in the park. Verifiable evidence may exist in NPSpecies, but it is not considered sufficient enough to elevate the status to Probably Present, nor current enough to elevate the status to Present. Efforts should be made to obtain current, verifiable evidence in NPSpecies to elevate the Park Status to "Present in Park". If reasonable efforts to obtain current, verifiable evidence are unsuccessful, then the Park Status should be changed to Historic, Encroaching, or False Report as applicable.
Encroaching	The species is not documented in the park, but is documented as being adjacent to the park and has potential to occur in the park.	Extremely low confidence that the organism is currently in the park, but extremely high confidence that the organism is currently adjacent to the park. Verifiable evidence may exist in NPSpecies documenting the occurrence in the park, but it is not current. Potential invasive organisms are good candidates for this Park Status designation, either before they enter a park or after they have been eliminated from a park.
Historic	Species' historical occurrence in the park is documented, but recent investigations indicate that the species is now probably absent.	Extremely low confidence that the organism is currently in the park. Verifiable evidence exists in NPSpecies, but is not current. Extinct, extirpated or eliminated species are candidates for a Historic *Park Status* designation.
False Report	Species previously reported to occur within the park, but current evidence indicates that the report was based on a misidentification, a taxonomic concept no longer accepted, or some other similar problem of interpretation.	Extremely low confidence that the organism is currently in the park. Evidence exists in NPSpecies, but it cannot be sufficiently verified.

21

Appendix (cont.). NPSpecies Data Dictionary

Abundance	The current abundance of each organism in each park.	Applicable only to organisms with the *Local List* checkbox checked and a *Park Status* of "Present". The values attempt to balance abundance with suitable habitat, and temporal/behavioral considerations. In practice, the entered value should apply (although there are numerous exceptions) to the abundance in the most suitable habitat of the organism, and at the time that the organism is engaged in it's principle behavior in (e.g. breeding, migrating, hibernating, etc.), or most important behavior to, the park. A future generation of NPSpecies will address the coding of *Abundance* (and associated *Residency*) to separate out the temporal and behavioral aspects. The Data Source field for Abundance is available to provide a citation that specifically addresses abundance in more detail.
Abundant		**Animals:** May be seen daily, in suitable habitat and season, and counted in relatively large numbers. **Plants:** Large number of individuals; wide ecological amplitude or occurring in habitats covering a large portion of the park.
Common		**Animals:** May be seen daily, in suitable habitat and season, but not in large numbers. **Plants:** Large numbers of individuals predictably occurring in commonly encountered habitats but not those covering a large portion of the
Uncommon		**Animals:** Likely to be seen monthly in appropriate season/habitat. May be locally common. **Plants:** Few to moderate numbers of individuals; occurring either sporadically in commonly encountered habitats or in uncommon habitats.
Rare		**Animals:** Present, but usually seen only a few times each year. **Plants:** Few individuals usually restricted to small areas of rare habitat.
Occasional		**Animals:** Occurs in the park at least once every few years, but not necessarily every year. **Plants:** Not applicable.
Unknown		Abundance unknown.

Residency	Current residency classification for each ANIMAL species in each park.	Applicable only to ANIMALS with the *Local List* checkbox checked and a *Park Status* of "Present". The values attempt to balance temporal and behavioral considerations. In practice, the entered value should apply (although there are numerous exceptions) to the residency of the organism at the time that the organism is engaged in its principle behavior (e.g. breeding, migrating, hibernating, etc.) in, or most important behavior to, the park. A future generation of NPSpecies will address the coding of Residency (and associated Abundance) to separate out the temporal and behavior aspects. The Data Source field for Residency is available to provide a citation that specifically addresses Residency in more detail.
Breeder		Population reproduces in the park.
Resident		A significant population is maintained in the park for more than two months each year, but it is not known to breed there.
Migratory		Migratory species that occurs in park approximately two months or less each year and does not breed there.
Vagrant		Park is outside of the species' usual range.
Unknown		Residency status in park is unknown.

Appendix (cont.). NPSpecies Data Dictionary

Nativity	Nativity classification for each organism for each park	Applicable only to organisms with the *Local List* checkbox checked. If the park-status of an organism is not "Present in Park", then nativity represents the nativity if the organism were eventually confirmed in the park.
	Native	Native The organism is native, or would be native, to the park (either endemic or indigenous).
	Non-native	The organism is not native, or would not be native, to the park (neither endemic nor indigenous).
	Unknown	Nativity status in the park is unknown.

The NPS has organized its parks with significant natural resources into 32 networks linked by geography and shared natural resource characteristics. The Heartland Network is composed of 15 National Park Service (NPS) units in eight Midwestern states. These parks contain a wide variety of natural and cultural resources including sites focused on commemorating civil war battlefields, Native American heritage, westward expansion, and our U.S. Presidents. The Network is charged with creating inventories of its species and natural features as well as monitoring trends and issues in order to make sound management decisions. Critical inventories help park managers understand the natural resources in their care while monitoring programs help them understand meaningful change in natural systems and to respond accordingly. The Heartland Network helps to link natural and cultural resources by protecting the habitat of our history.

The I&M program bridges the gap between science and management with a third of its efforts aimed at making information accessible. Each network of parks, such as Heartland, has its own multi-disciplinary team of scientists, support personnel, and seasonal field technicians whose system of online databases and reports make information and research results available to all. Greater efficiency is achieved through shared staff and funding as these core groups of professionals augment work done by individual park staff. Through this type of integration and partnership, network parks are able to accomplish more than a single park could on its own.

The mission of the Heartland Network is to collaboratively develop and conduct scientifically credible inventories and long-term monitoring of park "vital signs" and to distribute this information for use by park staff, partners, and the public, thus enhancing understanding which leads to sound decision making in the preservation of natural resources and cultural history held in trust by the National Park Service.

www.nature.nps.gov/im/units/htln/

Heartland
Network

Natural Resource Monitoring

The Department of the Interior protects and manages the nation's natural resources and cultural heritage; provides scientific and other information about those resources; and honors its special responsibilities to American Indians, Alaska Natives, and affiliated Island Communities.

NPS 394/100536, October 2009